MUSIC IN

ELIZABETHAN ENGLAND

By Dorothy E. Mason

PUBLISHED FOR

THE FOLGER SHAKESPEARE LIBRARY

University Press of Virginia

CHARLOTTESVILLE

ANY account of Elizabethan music, however brief, should note the fact that musical development in this age was part of a great intellectual and social movement that influenced the whole of life. The same forces that produced writers like Sir Philip Sidney, Edmund Spenser, William Shakespeare, Ben Jonson, John Donne, and Francis Bacon also produced musicians like William Byrd, Thomas Morley, Orlando Gibbons, Thomas Weelkes, and John Dowland. Artistic greatness was in the very air along with that exciting urge for adventure that was to widen the geographical horizons of the world, and men's spiritual concepts as well.

The great Queen, of course, provided an inspiration for the best efforts of Englishmen, whatever their aims and activities. For music she was the ideal patroness. No mean musician herself—she was an accomplished performer on the virginals—she aided her favorite art immensely in every way possible, bestowing her favors on the singers in chapel and court, on the musicians in public and private theatrical performances. To the great composers of her time she was particularly gracious and helpful.

When Elizabeth died in 1603, there was in England a large and active group of composers (including Byrd, Gibbons, Dowland, Pilkington, Weelkes, and Este among many others) who were destined to continue with brilliance the traditions of the sixteenth century well through the first quarter of the seventeenth. On the other hand, Thomas Tallis, whose music still remains a valuable heritage, had died in 1585, an aged man whose professional life had begun as a gentleman of the Chapel Royal of Henry VIII. Thus, we must keep in mind that the general term "Elizabethan music" is a broad one, covering a full century of distinguished musical activity.

This long chronological span means, of course, that there was no sudden outburst of song or of proficiency in producing or performing it in Elizabeth's age. Singing was an integral part of English life long before the beautifully planned and well-sung madrigals and airs had become a common heritage. We have record of the people, thousands of them, expressing their religious or patriotic fervor in song. In 1560, Bishop Jewel wrote to Peter Martyr:

A change appears more visible among the people; which nothing promotes more than the inviting them to sing Psalms. . . . Sometimes at Paul's Cross, there will be 6000 people singing together.°

Years later, long after the age with which we are now concerned was past, great throngs gathered in York Minster when that city was being besieged during the Civil War in 1644 and, according to Thomas Mace (*Musicks Monument*, 1676),

Always before the sermon the whole congregation sang a psalm, together with the choir and the organ. . . . When that vast concording unity of the whole congregational chorus came, as I may say, thundering in . . . I was so transported, and rapt up into high contemplations, that there was no room left in my whole man, *viz.* body, soul, and spirit, for anything below divine and heavenly raptures.

This glance at a century of communal enthusiasm for expression of devotion in song is presented only to emphasize the brilliance which Elizabeth's own age achieved, when all England was musically awake and literate. It is to this England we now turn.

We shall begin with a very brief survey of the music of the Church. There was a gradual transition from the services of the Roman Catholic Church to the final forms adopted for worship in the Church of England. The Roman plainsong was simplified; the Mass, in adapted form, became the service of Holy Communion. English was substituted for Latin, so that divine service might have meaning for all the people. The music of the Church of England consisted mainly of anthems, morning

---

° The spelling of this and all following quotations has been modernized.

and evening services [Plate 2], musical settings of the responses, and the litany. The anthems, while still contrapuntal in character, became more complex, though gloriously free-spirited and inspiring. Some of the finest of these were written by Christopher Tye, Orlando Gibbons, William Byrd, and Thomas Tallis. The Elizabethan settings of the Psalms which replaced the Catholic hymns were very moving and are still sung. During Elizabeth's reign, at least twenty-two psalters were published based on the metrical versions of the Psalms made by Sternhold and Hopkins alone, the first of them published with music in 1560. Distinguished Elizabethan composers of these settings included Robert Parsons, Thomas Tallis, John Cosyn, and William Damon [Plate 3]. With such inspiring music provided for them, we can understand the satisfaction that psalm-singing must have given Elizabeth's church-going subjects.

The chief glory of Elizabeth's age was, however, the development of its secular vocal music, which reached a high degree of artistry. It did so, of course, because the Elizabethans received perhaps even more enjoyment from singing together socially than they did from singing psalms together in church. An educated person of the time was expected to perform music more than just fairly well. Thomas Morley, "Bachelor of Musicke and Gentleman of Her Majesty's Royal Chapel," in his famous book on music and the teaching thereof, *A Plaine and Easie Introduction to Practicall Musicke* (1597), relates an imaginary conversation which took place at a supper party [Plate 4]:

Among the rest of the guests, by chance, master Aphron came thither also, who falling to discourse of music, was in an argument so quickly taken up and hotly pursued by Eudoxus and Calergus . . . as in his own art he was overthrown. But he still sticking in his opinion, the two gentlemen requested me to examine his reasons, and confute them. But I refusing and pretending ignorance, the whole company condemned me of discourtesy, being fully persuaded that I had been as skillful in that art as they took me to be learned in others. But supper being ended, and music books, according to the custom being brought to the table, the mistress of the house presented me with a part, earnestly requesting me to sing. But when, after many excuses, I protested unfainedly that I could not, every one began to wonder. Yea, some whispered to others, demanding how I was brought up.

We see implied here the prevalent idea that an educated man should not only be able to take his part in a madrigal, but also to know the niceties of musical theory. Moreover, Morley's evidence is supported by that of Henry Peacham, who wrote in *The Compleat Gentleman* in 1622 that one of the fundamental qualities of a gentleman was to be able "to sing your part sure, and at the first sight, withall, to play the same upon your viol, or the exercise of the lute," thus adding instrumental accomplishments to Morley's two earlier requirements.

About the musical interests of these people we have many other authentic reports. Contemporary records of all kinds, from royal account-books to household accounts, public documents, and private inventories, assure us that music, well learned and capably performed, was widespread throughout the land and an important part of everyday Elizabethan life. In addition to the masterpieces left by the greatest composers, we still have extant literally hundreds of catches, glees, ballads, street songs, and vendors' cries. They were sung or hummed on the street and played, with complicated variations, on the virginals by the well-trained sons and daughters of the higher gentry and nobility—all attesting to a land that was highly articulate in music.

The late Canon Fellowes, in his book on *The English Madrigal*, describes one of the great houses, of which there were many in England at this time, Hengrave Hall near Bury St. Edmunds. It was not by any means one of the largest or most beautiful, but it was ample and comfortable, having been built by Sir Thomas Kytson, a wealthy wool merchant who had a great trade with Antwerp. After two generations this family, thanks to shrewd marriages, occupied a place of social prominence and patronized the arts. The second Sir Thomas was particularly interested in music and encouraged performances in his house. Many documents concerning this household have been preserved and shed light on customs that were by no means confined to Hengrave Hall. One of the inventories made after the death of the younger Sir Thomas in 1602 reveals an astonishing music "establishment." There was "the chamber where the musicians play," and in this room were chests of instruments and many song books, English, Italian, and one from Spain. In all, some fifty-four books are listed, mainly of part-songs, for three, four, five, and six voices. There are also a few books of dance music: corrantos, pavans, and galliards. This is a remarkable list, particularly of song books, for most of the English madrigals had not as yet been published. Also on the list we find some forty instruments owned by the family, including twelve viols, seven recorders, four lutes, five virginals, various brasses and woodwinds, and two "great organs."

To have use for such a great number of instruments implies a fairly large group of players resident at the Hall. Their number would be supplemented on special occasions by professionals from the neighboring town of Bury St. Edmunds, by talented retainers, and now and then by guests who might have studied Morley's book.

Master of the music at Hengrave was none other than the famous madrigal composer, John Wilbye, who held his post there for many years. With such a leader, and with the library of at least fifty-four books, a goodly number of them being part-books, there must have been much singing—and good singing, too. Wilbye's music is not easy to perform. Neither were the Italian madrigals which were also there. Much of the music, particularly Wilbye's, was probably in manuscript and written for the Hall [Plate 5]. Wilbye's *First Set of English Madrigals,* published in 1598, was dated from the Austin Friars, the London home of the Kytsons, and dedicated to Sir Thomas Cavendish of Welbeck, who was the husband of Elizabeth, the eldest daughter of Sir Thomas. His second set, published in 1609, was dedicated to Lady Arabella Stuart, another relative of the Kytson family and an occasional visitor at Hengrave, where Wilbye doubtless met her.

This close family intimacy may explain one of the reasons for the charming freshness, the spontaneity, the verve of Wilbye's as well as of other English madrigals, qualities which were lacking in their continental counterpart, the Italian madrigal, upon which the English was modelled. The madrigal, which was a secular, lyrical poem in the native language, was set in the form of an *a capella* song, originally for three voices, and afterwards for four, five, or even more. This contrapuntal form was one which would naturally appeal to the English taste and to the English love for communal performance. The composers adopted what could have become a very artificial and sophisticated style, as it often was across the Channel, but they displayed so much enthusiasm and spontaneity, and were so greatly influenced by the lively spirit surrounding them, that the form became in their hands almost a native expression. Moreover, they seldom followed their Italian and French models in setting the songs to serious poetry, but instead chose popular verse, some of it based on matters of topical interest, such as Weelkes' madrigal called "The Andalusian Merchant," which reflects the common Elizabethan interest in travel and adventure, an eagerness expressed even in song:

> That Andalusian merchant that returns,
> > Laden with cochineal and China dishes,
> Reports in Spain, how strangely Fogo burns,
> > Amidst an ocean full of flying fishes.
> These things seem wondrous, yet more wondrous I,
> Whose heart with fear doth freeze, with love doth fry.

The later canzonets, airs, and ballads were far more consciously literary, and for these we find verses from England's great poets of the day: Sidney, Spenser, Shakespeare, Jonson, Donne, Raleigh, and others.

The terms "ayre" (air) and "canzonet" we often find used for the same sort of song—a composition for a single voice, with other voices or, later, instruments supporting it [Plate 6]. While the contrapuntal nature of the madrigal made it difficult to set more than one verse of a poem in any one song, the air was sufficiently simple in structure to permit many verses to be sung through without difficulty. For Hengrave Hall and like places, for groups of skilled performers or accomplished amateurs, the madrigal was a highly enjoyable form of entertainment. But at the turn of the century, when many poets were producing lyrics that fairly sang by themselves, it was inevitable that the more simple form of musical expression should become popular.

One of the most famous of the composers of airs was John Dowland, a singer *par excellence* and a lutenist without rival in his day. Of him Richard Barnfield wrote in his sonnet, "To his friend Maister R. L. in praise of Musique and Poetrie":

> Dowland to thee is dear, whose heavenly touch
> Upon the lute doth ravish human sense.

As may be deduced from the list of musical instruments at Hengrave Hall, the most popular ones were probably the lute, virginals, and the family of viols. These had already enjoyed a long popularity, for records tell us that Henry VIII had a large collection of them. The lute was a loved instrument among all classes, either played as a solo instrument for simple affecting airs or used in accompanying or supporting a solo voice. They were of various shapes and sizes, the commonest—the treble lute—being shaped like a large mandolin, with six strings, the five lower attached in pairs, making eleven in all. The strings were fretted and played by being plucked with the fingers of the right hand. The popularity of the instrument lasted until the very end of the seventeenth century [Plate 7].

The viols, too, were used both for solo and accompaniment. A chest of them, about which we read so much, consisted of two treble, two tenor, and two bass viols. If concerted music was played on a family, or chest, of viols, it was called a "consort." If some other instrument, such as a recorder or lute, was brought into the combination, it was known as a "broken consort," or "broken music" [Plate 8]. Viols had six strings, were fretted like the lute, and played with a bow [Plate 7]. The cittern, a kind of country cousin of the lute, usually had four wire strings and was played with a plectrum, or quill [Plate 9].

The virginal, one of the earliest of keyboard instruments, was rectangular in shape and had a keyboard of about four octaves, with strings plucked with a quill instead of being struck with a hammer like our modern piano [Plate 10]. It was queen of instruments during Elizabeth's reign, probably because she was known to be a very accomplished performer. She evidently took great pride in being so, for even in her later years diplomats were sometimes put to it to make the proper flattering remarks about the Queen's performance, even if it meant demeaning their own sovereign ladies.

Finally, we must at least mention the recorders, flutes, flageolets, rebecs (three-stringed "fiddles"), tabors (tiny drums), fifes, drums, and sackbuts (trombones)—all popular instruments since early days, and we hear of them repeatedly on the Elizabethan stage [Plates 1 and 9].

While much music was undoubtedly written for all these instruments (we still possess much, and over the centuries much more has undoubtedly been lost), yet performers could play from the part-song books just as well. Madrigals for voices often became the music for viols and lutes. Their composers even suggested such arrangements on the title-pages of their compositions: Michael Este, for example, notes his songs as "apt for viols and voices."

The printing of these part-song books "apt" for various combinations of voices and instruments should not be overlooked. As shown in Plates 6 and 11, the large folio volumes were so printed, and the parts so arranged, that several persons could sing or play from one book. For example, a work in four parts would usually be arranged thus: On the left-hand page was the cantus part, which, if it was also to be sung to the lute, would have the special lute tablature beneath it. On the right-hand page the three parts were arranged so that the performers could sit or stand at three sides of the table: at the bottom of the page was the tenor part; at the top, facing the other way, the altus; between them, and facing both, was the bassus. In some books, such as Leighton's [Plate 11], alternative instruments were definitely suggested by the composers themselves, making a "broken consort" performance. The polyphony of the part-song easily lent itself to the light-toned instruments of the period, the viols, lutes, and gambas.

In 1599 Thomas Morley published one of the first instrumental ensemble compositions, the *Consort Lessons*, written for six instruments: treble lute, pandora (a kind of lute), cittern, bass viol, flute, and treble viol. Thomas Weelkes, Orlando Gibbons, Tobias Hume, and John Dowland were also among the prominent writers of vocal music who used their polyphonic gifts in the writing of fantasias for instruments and voices.

Weelkes and Gibbons, along with Richard Deering, really had some fun with the form, too, for together they incorporated into one such fantasy more than one hundred and fifty cries and songs of the itinerant vendors on London's streets. All the individual songs concerned themselves with such matters as "New oysters, new mussels, my lily-white mussels," "Hot mutton pies," and "Cherry-ripe, strawberry ripe." Weelkes, amusingly enough, added a rather lugubrious "Alleluia" to all his pieces in this delightful collection.

This could be called "art music" with popular elements, since it was done with consummate skill by England's finest and most accomplished musicians and composers. The real "folk music," performed on the streets along with the cries of the vendors, by ballad-singers, itinerant fiddlers, and others less accomplished, was another thing, no less interesting. Great numbers of ballad texts were printed with directions to be sung to such-and-such an air, "Greensleeves," for example. These ballads were enormously popular, for references to them are constant in all types of written records, from pulpit to theatre. We are reminded of Mrs. Ford in *The Merry Wives of Windsor* [II.i.55 ff.]:

I shall think the worst of fat men as long as I have an eye to make difference of men's liking. And yet he would not swear; prais'd women's modesty, and gave such orderly and well-behaved reproof to all uncomeliness that I would have sworn his disposition would have gone to the truth of his words. But they do no more adhere and keep place together than the Hundred Psalm to the tune of "Greensleeves."

In a manuscript commonplace book once belonging to John Dowland, there is a version of this ballad set for lute, another indication of its popularity amongst all people at the time [Plate 12]. Many ballads and other forms of then-current "popular" music are still accessible to us in Thomas Ravenscroft's collections: *Pammelia* (1609), *Deuteromelia* (1609), and *Melismata* (1611).

Since the printing of complex musical texts had not reached so high an art in England as on the Continent, most of the enormous amount of virginal music written at this time was circulated in manuscript. Two notable exceptions are the *Parthenia, or Maydenhead of the first musicke that euer was printed for the Virginals. Composed by three famous Masters William Byrd, Dr. John Bull and Orlando Gibbons Gentilmen of his Maiesties most Illustrious Chappell,* printed from engraved plates in 1611; and its companion volume, *Parthenia Inviolata or Mayden-Musicke for the Virginall and Bass-Violl. Selected out of the Compositions of the most famous in that Arte by Robert Hole and consecrated to all true Louers & Practicers thereof.* In recent years much more of this interesting music for a very beautiful instrument is being printed for the first time and regaining a deserved admiration.

Music had an important part in the early dramas. The mystery and miracle plays popular in England in the fourteenth century were still being acted occasionally early in Elizabeth's reign and were another means of preserving and continuing the folk-art of the people. Early interludes also continued the tradition, for many of them specifically indicated the use of songs and even particular instruments. John Redford, musician and playwright (*ca.*1485–*ca.*1545), in his position as choir-master of St. Paul's, London, would have been in charge of many of the Latin plays presented by the choir-boys for visiting dignitaries. An extant manuscript of his morality, *Wyt and Science,* contains the words of three different songs. At the end of the play is a further note: "Here come in four with viols and sing 'remembrance,' and at the last quire [verse] all make cur[t]sey and so go forth singing." At the end of another morality play,

Redford again uses music: "Here the[y] sing 'Hey nonny, nonny,' and so go forth singing." We meet that particular refrain long afterwards in Elizabethan ballets.

In 1562 the famous tragedy of *Gorboduc* was acted in the Hall of the Inner Temple on Twelfth Night, and the play was produced with musical effects supplied by viols, cornets, oboes, drums, and flutes. This was no exceptional presentation. Music like this was expected in a play, for it was an important and integral part of everyday life even this early, and actors were already well equipped, musically, to depict that life upon the stage.

With the growth of interest in theatrical performances, with recognized stage practices, there came into being certain accepted standards of stage music as well. The Theatre, built in 1576, and its neighboring houses were repertory theatres, producing a different play each acting day. As we learn from Henslowe's *Diary*, in a typical two-weeks' schedule for February, 1596, the Admiral's Men presented ten plays on twelve acting days, each play employing from ten to twenty musical effects. In the public theatres, music was probably placed in the same category as the stage properties, such as costumes and the machines, to be used whenever required by the dramatic texts. Records show that in 1598 the Lord Admiral's Company owned three trumpets, one drum, one treble viol, one bass viol, one pandora, one sackbut, three tymbrels (small drums), and bells. Considering the demands of the texts of the plays and the instruments in each theatre, there must have been a need for at least eight musicians in each company.

From the play texts themselves we learn that music of certain kinds had specific meanings for the Elizabethan audience. When a king entered or left the stage, hoyboyes (oboes) sounded. A drum beaten on or off stage could indicate a marching army. For each phase of the stage battles there was special music—such as "alarum," "parley," "retreat," played by trumpet and drum, and sometimes even by the flute. Likewise, certain dramatic situations had corresponding musical formulas. It is evident that these were taken from everyday Elizabethan life.

Trumpets and kettledrums were the signs apparent of the approach of Elizabeth and her court and thus heralded the Queen on all state occasions. Parenthetically, it may be stated here that Elizabeth loved the sound of drums and trumpets, and as early as 1571 maintained eighteen trumpeters and six sackbut players in her household. Every day the signal for dinner was given by twelve trumpets and a pair of drums, which "made the hall ring for half an hour together."

Shakespeare, along with his fellow-dramatists, called for much music in his plays. One critic writes: "Shakespeare knew his audience well, and it cannot be coincidence that the two plays whose titles imply that he was giving it what it wanted contain the most songs. *As You Like It* and *Twelfth Night, or What You Will* contain no fewer than six songs each." Two pages sing "It was a lover and his lasse" in *As You Like It* [see Plate 13 for Morley's setting of this song; it may have been the version sung in the play]. Ophelia sings in *Hamlet,* Desdemona in *Othello.* Robert Johnson's settings of "Full fathom five" and "Where the bee sucks" from the *Tempest* may have been written for the first performance of the play, although they were not published until 1660 by Dr. John Wilson [Plates 14 and 15]. "What shall he have that kill the deere," a catch sung in *As You Like It* [IV.ii.10–7], comes down to us recorded in a seventeenth century manuscript book of catches [Plate 16].

It must be stressed that all of these songs were not what we now might call incidental music, but that the playwrights used music as a deliberate device to suggest moods, provide atmosphere, prepare the spectators for coming action, and emphasize dramatic situations. Of course, it supplied extraneous entertainment as well.

Our most important generalization to be made about this constant and significant use of music is that the English theatre was musical because the English audience was musically literate, delighted in music, and demanded it. We must remember, too, that the love of music in the plays had received an impetus from the boy choirs, particularly those of the Chapel Royal. It had been customary from early times for the Children of the

Chapel, as they were called, to take part in dramatic entertainment. By the 1570's enterprising Masters of the Chapel Royal were using the boys almost as professional players, and it was logical to emphasize music when the actors themselves were so well equipped to provide such entertainment. Henry VIII and Elizabeth often availed themselves of the talents of the boys of their Chapel, and in many a record we find in the court orders to the Lord Chamberlain the words, "The children of the Chapel to come before the Queen at dinner with a carol."

In 1602 a German visitor, Frederic Gershow, touring England with his master the Duke of Stettin, was greatly impressed by the Queen's Children of the Chapel, and wrote:

The Queen maintains a number of young boys who are required to devote themselves earnestly to the art of singing, and to learn to perform on various sorts of musical instruments, and at the same time to carry on their studies. These boys have their special preceptors in all the various arts, and in particular excellent instructors in music. . . . For a whole hour preceding the play one listens to a delightful musical entertainment on organs, lutes, and flutes.

In addition to these boys, Elizabeth had at her disposal for special occasions, or for special music at theatrical performances at court, many other well-trained London musicians, including the "musicians of the city," or the Lord Mayor's Waits. It is interesting to note that Thomas Morley's *Consort Lessons* (1599), previously mentioned, and one of the few collections of instrumental pieces in print this early, was dedicated to the Lord Mayor and his Waits. They must have been a varied and accomplished group, considering the variety of instruments called for in Morley's score. His dedication is both flattering and significant:

As the ancient custom of this most honourable and renowned city hath been ever to retain and maintain excellent and expert musicians to adorn your Honour's favours, feasts, and solemn meetings; to those your Lordship's Waits, after commending these my labours to your honourable patronage, I recommend the same to your servants' careful and skillful handling, that the wants of exquisite harmony, apparent, being left unsupplied for brevity of proportions, may be excused by their melodious additions, purposing hereafter to give them more testimony of my love towards them.

This means that Morley had indicated the general progressions he wished, and the ornamentation of that very simply indicated melody was left up to the skill and good taste of the various performers. Perhaps they had studied his book, and he felt confident of their ability to do his great work simple justice.

In public theatres music was often performed after the play in addition to such music as may have been a part of the drama. We have an eyewitness, one Paul Hentzner, a Brandenburg jurist, who visited London in 1598 and reported:

Without the city there are some theatres where English actors represent almost every day tragedies and comedies to very numerous audiences; these are concluded with music, variety of dances, and the excessive applause of those that are present.

One of the most popular Elizabethan entertainers was Shakespeare's fellow-actor, Will Kemp, who was famous both in England and on the Continent for his jigs, which were part dance, part pantomime, part songs. Rude things they probably were, but they appealed to the sense of humor of a people who also delighted in bear-baiting and the performances of the dancing horse. After the tours of the English companies on the Continent, many imitations of English plays and jigs appeared there, particularly in Germany. The vogue for them lasted long in England. In one of the late editions (ca.1725) of the mid-seventeenth century popular *Dancing Master*, first published by John Playford, there is a dance, with the music, entitled "Kemp's jigg" [Plate 17]. These jigs and suchlike entr'actes gave to the general public the variety of amusement and spectacle which private audiences enjoyed in a far more elegant, rich, and subtle fashion in the masques.

The masque was a form of courtly entertainment which had the characteristics of both play and opera. Its plot was unfolded in song and spoken words, with singing by solo voices and chorus and much intricate dancing, all performed against a gorgeously decorative background, with complicated machinery and effective tableaux designed by the greatest artists of the day. The beginnings of the masque go back to the fourteenth century, but its real development started in the last years of Elizabeth and culminated during the reigns of her two successors. Very little of the music written for the masques has survived in print—probably much of it was never printed, since the performances were given only privately at the court or in noblemen's houses. Thomas Campion's *Description of a Maske: Presented in the Banqueting Roome at Whitehall, on St. Stephens night . . .* (1614) is one of the few printed masques that have come down to us [Plates 18 and 19].

In concluding this brief description of Elizabethan music, it is fitting that we pay tribute to the great Queen who was an ever-constant inspiration to the musicians of her time. We like to think of Elizabeth on one of her "progresses," say the one at Elvetham in 1591, when her host, Lord Hertford, provided music for her pleasure.

On the day of the Queen's departure, there was another "song of six parts with the music of an exquisite consort," to words beginning *Eliza is the fairest Queen.* During this performance, "the Queen of Fairies . . . danced and sang before Her Majesty," who insisted on the performance being repeated three times over, and "called for divers Lords and Ladies to behold it." And finally, "as Her Majesty passed through the park gate, there was a consort of musicians hidden in a bower, to whose playing this ditty of *Come again,* was sung, with excellent division, by two that were cunning. . . . As this song was sung, Her Majesty, notwithstanding the great rain, stayed her coach and pulled off her mask, giving great thanks."

When Elizabeth was old and pathetic and failing, two years before her death, twenty-three of the greatest composers of her realm paid her a touching tribute; together they composed that magnificent set of madrigals in her honor, *The Triumphes of Oriana* (1601), each song ending with the refrain, "Long live Oriana," a lyrical echo of the shouted *vivat*'s that had rung in her ears when she ascended the throne forty-three long years before [Plate 20].

SUGGESTED READING

Sir George Grove, *Dictionary of Music and Musicians* (5th edition, ed. Eric Blum, 9 vols., London, 1954) contains invaluable information about music, musical instruments, development of musical forms, and composition, as well as interesting biographical material for the Tudor period.

Morrison Comegys Boyd, *Elizabethan Music and Musical Criticism* (Philadelphia, 1940); an indispensable book for this period with its broad study of the development of Tudor music in all its manifestations.

Edmund H. Fellowes, an authority on Elizabethan music, has written many books on the period, including *English Cathedral Music* (London, 1941); *The English Madrigal* (London, 1925); *The English Madrigal Composers* (Oxford, 1921); *The English Madrigal School* (36 vols., London, 1913–24); *The English School of Lutenist Song Writers* (16 vols., London, 1920–23); *Orlando Gibbons and his Family* (London, 1951); *William Byrd* (London, 1936).

William H. G. Flood, *Early Tudor Composers* (London, 1925); useful for the early years of the sixteenth century (1485–1555).

For music of the theatre, Sir Frederick Bridge, *Shakespearean Music in the Plays and Early Operas* (London, 1923); George H. Cowling, *Music on the Shakespearean Stage* (Cambridge, 1913); Louis C. Elson, *Shakespeare in Music* (Boston, 1901); Fellowes' edition of the *Songs & Lyrics from the Plays of Beaumont and Fletcher* (London, 1928).

William Chappell, *Old English Popular Music* (London, 1893) is still indispensable for folk music.

Information on musical instruments and music written for them may be found in Charles van den Borren, *Sources of Keyboard Music in England* (London, 1915); Francis W. Galpin, *A Textbook of European Musical Instruments* (London, [1946]); Margaret H. Glyn, *About Elizabethan Virginal Music and Its Composers* (London, [n.d.]); Max Kenyon, *Harpsichord Music* (London, 1949); Gerald R. Hayes, *Musical Instruments and Their Music* (2 vols., London, 1928–30).

Gustav Reese, *Music in the Renaissance* (London, [1954]) should be read for its broad knowledge of all Renaissance music, of which the English, however important, was only a part.

An Elizabethan Song Book, the music edited by Noah Greenberg, the text by W. H. Auden and Chester Kallman (London, 1954); a collection of many of the most interesting and beautiful Tudor songs. This is also available in a paper-backed edition, published by Doubleday in 1954.

Musica Britannica (15 vols., 2 still in preparation, London, 1951–) is a national collection of British music from the Middle Ages through the eighteenth century. This includes much hitherto unpublished material—music for the early Church and instrumental and vocal collections of the Tudor period, as well as masques, operas, and chamber music of the later period.

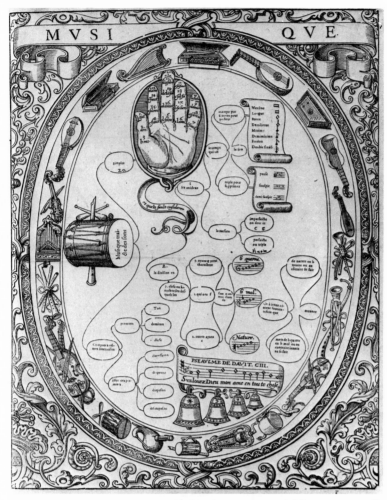

Plate 1. "Musique." From Christophe de Savigny, *Tableaux accomplis de tous les arts liberaux*, Paris, 1587.

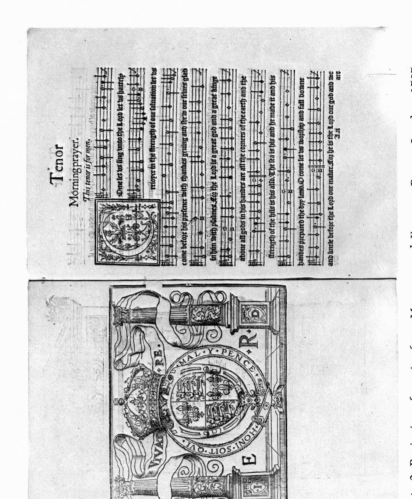

Morningprayer.

This tenor is for men.

Come let vs sing vnto the Lord let vs hartily reioyce in the strength of our saluation let vs come before his presence with thankes geuing and shew our selues glad in him with psalmes. For the Lord is a great god and a great kinge aboue all gods in this handes are all the corners of the earth and the strength of the hilles is his also. The sea is his and he made it and his handes prepared the dry lande. O come let vs worship and fall downe and knele before the Lord our maker. For he is the Lord our god and we are the

H.ii.

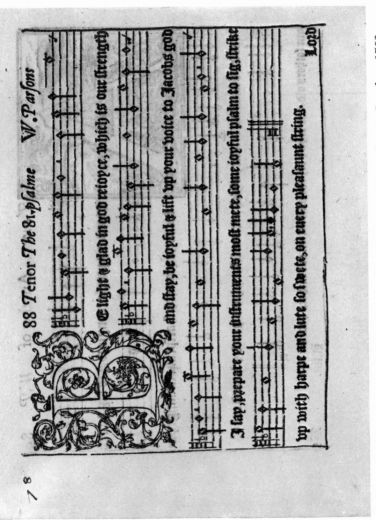

Plate 3. The 81st Psalm from *The Whole Psalmes in Foure Partes*, London, 1563.

Plate 4. Title-page of Thomas Morley's *A Plaine and Easie Introduction to Practicall Musicke*, London, 1597.

Plate 5. A manuscript copy of a song by John Wilbye in a music commonplace book.

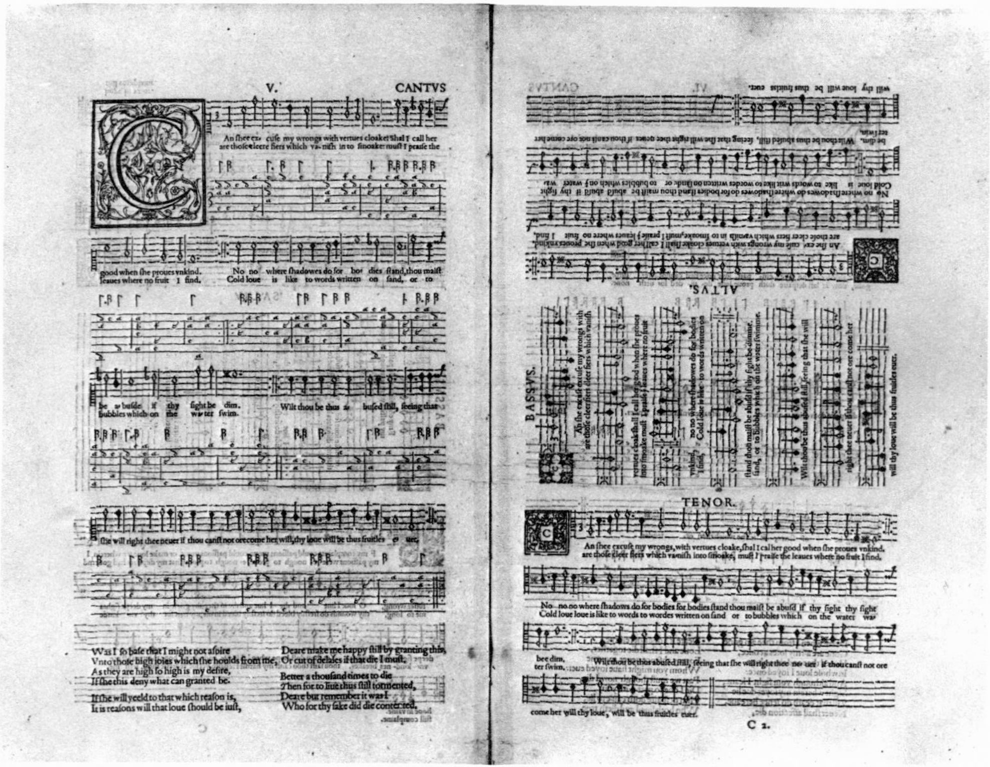

Plate 6. An air from John Dowland's *First Booke of Songes or Ayres,* London, 1600.

24

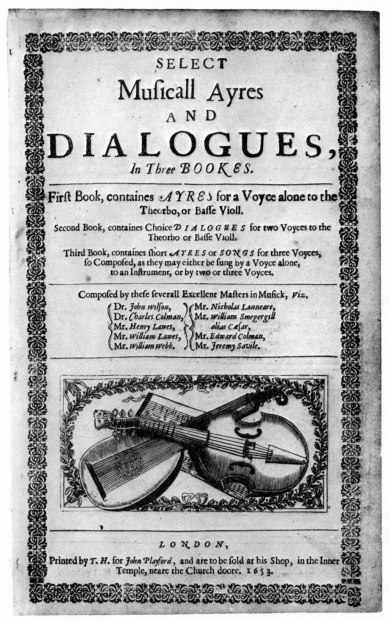

SELECT
Muſicall Ayres
AND
DIALOGUES,
In Three BOOKES.

First Book, containes *AYRES* for a Voyce alone to the Theorbo, or Baſſe Violl.

Second Book, containes Choice *DIALOGUES* for two Voyces to the Theorbo or Baſſe Violl.

Third Book, containes ſhort *AYRES* or *SONGS* for three Voyces, ſo Compoſed, as they may either be ſung by a Voyce alone, to an Inſtrument, or by two or three Voyces.

Compoſed by theſe ſeverall Excellent Maſters in Muſick, *Viz.*

Dr. *John Wilſon*,   Mr. *Nicholas Lanneare*,
Dr. *Charles Colman*,   Mr. *William Smegergill*
Mr. *Henry Lawes*,   *alias Cæſar*,
Mr. *William Lawes*,   Mr. *Edward Colman*,
Mr. *William Webb*.   Mr. *Jeremy Savile*.

LONDON,

Printed by *T. H.* for *John Playford*, and are to be ſold at his Shop, in the Inner Temple, neare the Church doore. 1653.

Plate 7. Lute and viol. From John Playford's *Select Musicall Ayres and Dialogues*, London, 1653.

Plate 8. Dancing in early Venice to the music of a "broken consort" of viols and lute. From Giacomo Franco's *Habiti d'huomeni et donne Venetia*, [1626].

Musical Instruments. C. Instrumenta Musica.

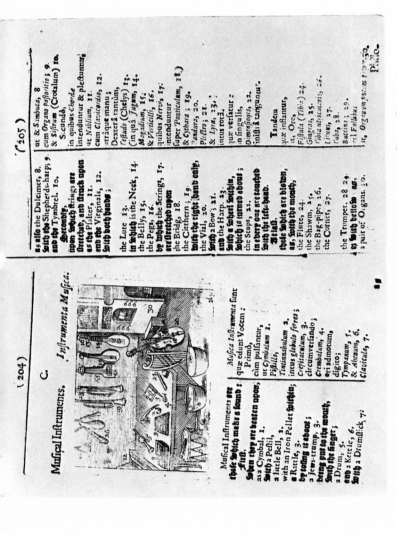

Musical Instruments are those which make a sound:
First,
Such as they are beaten upon;
as a Cymbal, 1.
with a Pestil,
a little Bell, 2.
with an Iron Pellet within;
a Rattle, 3.
by tossing it about;
a Jews-trump, 3.
being put to the mouth,
with the finger;
a Drum, 5.
and a Kettle, 6.
with a Drumstick, 7;

Musica Instrumenta sunt
quæ edunt Vocem:
Primò,
cum pulsantur,
ut Cymbalum 1.
Pistillo,
Tintinnabulum 2.
intus globulo ferreo;
Crepitaculum, 3.
circumversando;
Crembalum, 4.
ori admotum,
digito;
Tympanum, 5.
& Ahenum, 6.
Claviculæ, 7.

as also the Dulcimer, 8.
with the Shepherds-harp, 9.
and the Tymbrel, 10.
Secondly,
upon which strings are
stretched, and struck upon
as the Psalter, 11.
and the Virginals, 12.
with both hands;

the Lute 13.
in which is the Neck, 14.
the Belly, 15.
the Pegs, 16.
by which the Strings, 17.
are stretched upon
the Bridg, 18.
the Cithern; 19.
the Bridg, 18.
with the right hand only,
the Vial, 20.
with a Bow; 21.
and the Harp. 23.
with a sobœl Scutchin,
which is turned about ;
the Stops, 22.
in every one are touched
with the left-hand.
Thirdly,
those which are blown,
as, with the mouth,
the Flute, 24.
the Shawm, 2 [...]
the Bag-pipe, 16.
the Cornet, 27.

the Trumpet, 28 29.
or with bellows as.
a pair of Organs, 30.

ut & Sambuca, 8
cum Organo Pastoritio ; 9.
& Sistrum (Crotalum) 10.
Secundò,
in quibus Chordæ
intenduntur & plectuntur;
ut Nablium, 11.
cum Clavicordio, 12.
utrâque manu;
Dexterâ tantùm,
Testudo (Chelys) 13.
(in quâ Jugum, 14.
Magadium, 15.
& Verticilli, 16.
quibus Nervi 17.
intenduntur
super Ponticulum, 18.)
& Cithara ; 19.
Pandura, 20.
Plectro ; 21.
& Lyra, 23. ;
intus rota,
quæ vertatur:
in singulis,
Dimensiones, 22.
sinistrâ tanguntur.
Tandem
quæ inflantur,
ut, Ore,
Fistula (Tibia) 24.
Gingras, 25.
tibia utricularis, 26.
Lituus, 27.
Tuba, 28.
Buccina ; 29.
vel Follibus
ut, Organum pneumaticum, 30.

Plate 9. Musical instruments of Elizabeth's age. From Johann Comenius, *Orbis sensualium pictus,* 1685.

THE
Banquet of MUSICK:
OR,

A Collection of the newest and best SONGS
sung at Court, and at Publick Theatres.

WITH

A THOROW-BASS for the *Theorbo-Lute*,
Bass-Viol, *Harpsichord*, or *Organ*.

Composed by several of the Best Masters.

The WORDS by the *Ingenious Wits* of this Age.

THE FIRST BOOK.

LICENSED,
Nov. 19. 1687.   *Rob. Midgley.*

In the SAVOY.
Printed by E. *Jones*, for *Henry Playford*, at his Shop near the *Temple* Church, 1688.

Plate 10. Virginals and viol. From Henry Playford's *Banquet of Musick*,
London, 1688.

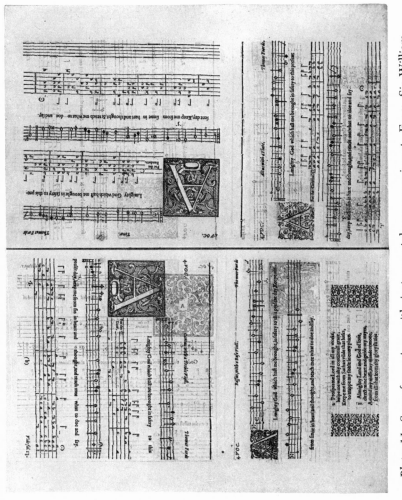

Plate 11. Song for voices with instrumental accompaniment. From Sir William Leighton's *The Teares or Lamentations of a Sorrowfull Soule,* London, 1614.

29

the the treble to gren sluis

the ground to gren sluis

Plate 12. A manuscript commonplace book, partly in the hand of John Dowland.

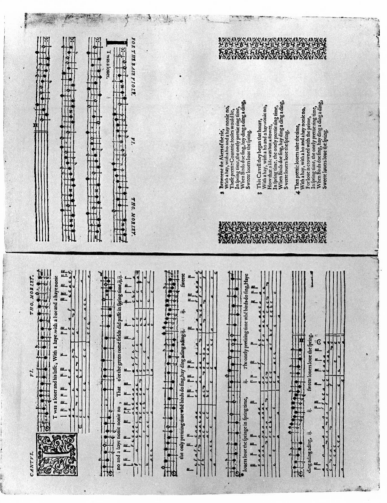

Plate 13. A song from Thomas Morley's First Book of Ayres, London, 1600.

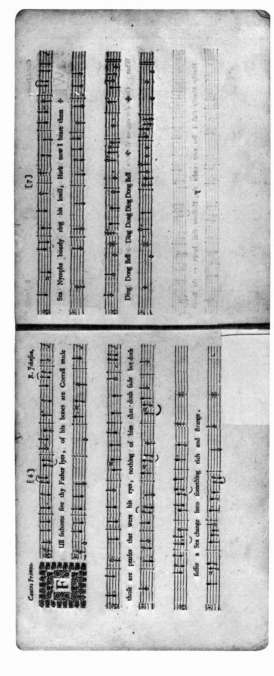

Plate 14. Song from Shakespeare's *Tempest* printed in Dr. John Wilson's *Cheerful Ayres or Ballads*, Oxford, 1660.

32

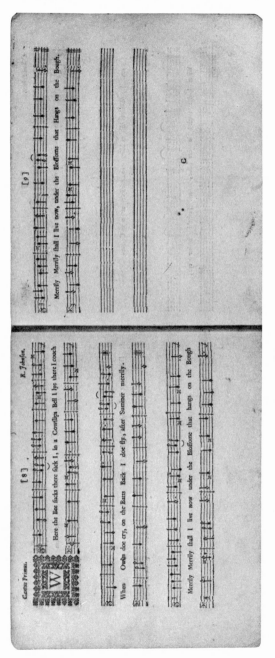

Plate 15. Song from *The Tempest* printed in Dr. John Wilson's *Cheerfull Ayres or Ballads.*

Plate 16. A mid-17th-century manuscript commonplace book containing settings of Shakespeare's songs.

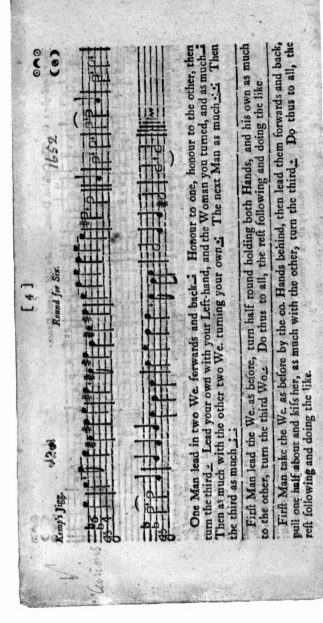

[4]

Kemp's Jigg.

Round for Six.

One Man lead in two We. forwards and back — Honour to one, honour to the other, then turn the third — Lead your own with your Left-hand, and the Woman you turned, and as much — Then as much with the other two We. turning your own — The next Man as much — Then the third as much —

First Man lead the We. as before, turn half round holding both Hands, and his own as much to the other, turn the third Wo— Do thus to all, the rest following and doing the like.

First Man take the We. as before by the co. Hands behind, then lead them forwards and back, pull one half about and kiss her, as much with the other, turn the third — Do thus to all, the rest following and doing the like.

Plate 17. A jig from John Playford's Dancing-Master, 18th edition, [ca. 1725].

The discription of a Maske

Chorus.

Vanish, vanish hence confusion,
Dimme not Hymens goulden light
With false illusion.
The Fates shall doe him right,
And Fame Eternise,
Who passe through all enchauntments free.

Eternitie singes alone.

Braue may this Sacred Tree,
The Tree of Grace, and Bountie,
Set in Bel-Annas eye.
For sho, sho, only sho,
Can all Knotted spels vnty,
Puld from the Stocke, no bor blast Hands remoue
To any suppliant Hand, a bough,
And let that Hand advance it now
Against a Charme, that Charme shall fade away.

Toward the ende of this Song the three, definitiuely set the Tree of Golde before the Queene.

Chorus.

Since Knightly valour rescues Dames distressed,
By Fortunes Dames, lot charm'd Knights bereleased.

After

---

on St. Stephens night.

After this Chorus, one of the Squires speakes.

SInce Knight by valour Relieue Dames distresse,
Let them be by the Queene of Dames releast:
So sing the Destinyes, who neuer erre,
Fixing this Tree of Grace and Botruite heere,
From which, for our enchaunted Knights we craue
A branche, puld by your Sacred Hand, to haue
That we may beare it as the Faces distre,
And manifest your glory in the flock,
In vertues fauour then, and Pittie now,
(Great Queene) vouchsafe vs diuine touch of bough.

At the end of this speech, the Queene puld a branch from the Tree and gaue it to a Nobleman who deli-
uered it to one of the Squires.

A Song whilst the Squires descend
With the bough, toward the Scene.

Goe happy man lik th' Euening Starre,
Whose beames to Bride-groomes well-come are;
May neither Hagge, nor Friend with stand
The power of thy Victorious Hand,
The Vncharm'd a Knights surrender now,
By vertue of thy raised Bough.

Away Enchantments, Vanish quite,
No more delay our longing sight:
'Tis fruitlesse to contend with Fate,
Who giues vs pow're against your hate,
Braue Knights, in Countrey pomp appeare,
For now are you long lookt for heere.

B 2   Then

Plate 18. Two pages from Thomas Campion's The Description of a Maske: Presented in the Banqueting Roome at Whitehall, on Saint Stephens night last, at the Mariage of the Right Honourable the Earle of Somerset: and the right noble the Lady Frances Howard, London, 1614.

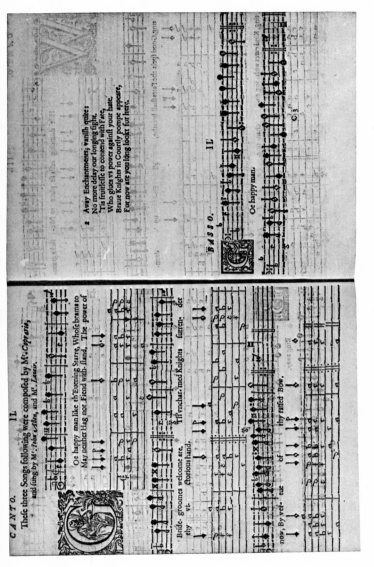

Plate 19. A song from Campion's Description of a Maske.

37

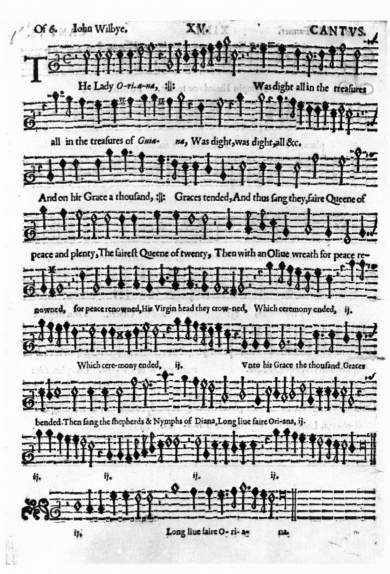

Plate 20. John Wilbye's contribution to Thomas Morley's collection of madrigals, *The Triumphes of Oriana,* London, 1601.

T   72   5